SCARS

How To be Healed From Brokenness

DR. RONN HALE

Unless otherwise indicated, all Scripture quotations are taken from the King James Version of the Bible.

Scriptures quotations marked (NKJV) are taken from the New King James Version of the Holy Bible, (NLT) are taken from the New Living Translation of the Holy Bible, (AMP) are taken from the Amplified Version of the Holy Bible, (ASV) are taken from the American Standard Version of the Holy Bible, (ESV) are taken from the English Standard Version of the Holy Bible and (AMPC) are taken from the Amplified Bible, Classic Edition.

Copyright © 2019 by Ronn Hale Ministries
P.O Box1208
Litchfield Park, Az 8530
Printed in the United States of America.

ISBN : 978-1-9161791-8-9

Published by:
Gracehouse Publishing
56, Gosport Road, Walthamstow,
London, United Kingdom, E17 7LY

All rights reserved under any and all applicable International Copyright Law. The contents and cover of this book may not be reproduced in whole or in part in any form without the express written consent of author or Ronn Hale Ministries.

Contents

Dedication

TO MY HEAVENLY FATHER, my Lord, Jesus Christ, and the precious Holy Spirit for being the ingenuity leading me to wholeness. To my beautiful, anointed, and faithful wife, Donneta Hale, who walks alongside me as a partner in advancing the Kingdom of God. To our three sons, Ronnie III, Dallas and Christian, God's future generals. To my beautiful grandchildren Ronnie IV, Amaya and Christian Jr.

I want to honor my mother, Marilyn Cook, who always spoke words of encouragement to me that built my confidence. To my father, Ronnie Hale Sr., who has now gone to be with the Lord, but, in his later years spoke into my life helping me become a better man of God. To my beloved Aunt Delores for loving me like one of her own children. To my in-laws, Paul and Ruby Banks, for guidance and inspiration. To the rest of my family for loving me for who I am.

Thank you to my spiritual sons and daughters, The Carpenter's House family, for the support and believing in me. A special thanks to Gabriela Jimenez, Cara Clayton, and Lincoln Harris for editing and helping to structure what God gave me.

To all the scarred and brokenhearted Christians…May you be restored to wholeness, so that you can walk in the fullness of your anointing and bring glory to our Heavenly Father.

Introduction

FOR THOSE WHO DO not know me, I am a very passionate teacher. Everything I teach is based upon the Word of God and the journey of my life. My desire is to build up the Body of Christ with the infallible Word of God. I believe that we're living in a day that God is about to expose potentials that have been lying dormant in your life.

Did you know that God wants you to be whole? He doesn't just want us to be healed and restored, He wants us WHOLE in everything. That's what Jesus came to do, to restore man back to His original state. That man would not only have dominion, but that he would have peace of mind and the wisdom of God, and be led, as Adam was supposed to be led, by the Holy Spirit.

Many people have a tendency of hiding their scars by pretending they're happy. They're living in a world of false realities and, with false realities, comes a certain sense of shame. However, in order to reach the level that you were meant to go to, you must confront the scars in your life. By not attempting to become your best, you rob the world of your external contribution, and it robs you of internal fulfillment.

Often times, we all have encountered different individuals who try to identify you based on where you came from. They try to name you by the events that have occurred in your life. Over the course of my life, beginning when I was a young boy, I was identified as a person who would never advance, due to what appeared to be a lack of understanding in school. They gave me the label of a "person with special needs," and they put me in the Special Education program. They said I would never be able to advance in life, because "I was slow to process." I carried that label, "special needs person," up until the seventh grade. Even the teachers had concluded that I would never be successful. Hearing them refer me to this label, cut me, leaving me scarred. When negative things are spoken about you, they wound you deeply. Externally, no one could see how deeply I was scarred from these words that were spoken over my life, but I truly believed that what they had said, would be the result of my future.

There are probably people in your life who have identified you a certain way and have been verbally abusive to you. For example, they have said things to you like, "Why can't you be smarter?"; "What's wrong with you?"; "Why can't you be like your sister?"; "Why can't you be like your brother?"; "You act just like your father!"; "Why can't you be intelligent?"; and "You will never advance in life if you do this!" All these words cause scars! If you allow the words and the opinions of others to dictate your future, you will find yourself in the place of stagnation.

The only way you can really become what God sees you to be, is if you come to admit that those things have indeed hurt you. I know Pastors, leaders, Bishops and Bishops' wives that are scarred and wounded within, but on the outside, they hide it by walking around smiling and acting as if nothing is wrong. This cannot continue if we're expecting God to advance our lives. Healing begins at the point of exposure. However, the spirit of pride hinders individuals, from admitting that things have scarred and hurt them. Instead of admitting their woundedness and asking God for complete wholeness, they have a tendency of covering it up by plastering a fake smile on their face and moving on.

Proverbs 18:14 (NKJV) says,

> ***"The spirit of a man will sustain his infirmity; but a wounded spirit who can bear?"***

I have never met an unscarred person, or someone who has not been heartbroken at least once in their life. It happens with life's journey. With the rise of mental health concerns,

I felt it necessary to open up on things that people do not like to talk about: i.e., the end of an intimate relationship, verbal abuse, unforgiveness, rejection, and feeling lost or unimportant. We live in a world with flawed humans who fail us, make mistakes and scar us. This book will allow people to understand that they are not alone, and that there is a light at the end of the tunnel. Mental barriers can be overcome, confidence regained, and scars and broken hearts healed.

CHAPTER 1

HOW TO IDENTIFY WHEN YOU ARE SCARRED

WHEN YOU CANNOT MOVE ON…

YOU REFLECT ON YOUR former years, and see a history filled with people who have hurt or offended you. When you are scarred, this gradually conditions your mind to believe that there is nothing positive in your future. NOT believing that you CAN, is the biggest trap of them all. When you do not know your own greatness is possible, you don't bother attempting to move ahead. All too often, we let the rejections and scars of our past dictate every move we make, and we do not allow ourselves to be any better than what some opinionated person or narrow circumstance once told us was true. Of course, being rejected doesn't mean you aren't good enough! It just means the other person, or circumstance, failed to align with what God has given you to offer to the world. You have become a victim of someone else's view of you.

Anytime someone brings up their past, it indicates that they are scarred, because they have not been able to forget what was spoken over them. Many times, the people speaking negatively into your life are the people who are supposed to be overseers that are called to help you move forward, but because of their own scars, they are unable to. Because of their scars, they repeat what they heard spoken into them. Most of the people that you have been scarred by, are those whom you trusted, such as your spouse, child, mother, father, sibling or a co-worker. It could even have been a school system that said you were a special needs person and that you couldn't comprehend teaching, which made you feel as if you would never achieve anything in life.

If many of these people spoke death over your life and said, "You will never progress!", or "You will always be this way!", it would scar you, leading you to the point where you cannot move on and you find yourself continually speaking about the issues of your former years, and everything you are trying to do doesn't work. Then again, those nagging and gnawing things in your past hinder you, and you reflect back on the decisions you have made, and, who or what, may have put you in a place or position that you should not be in. The more you come in relationship with God, the less toxic thoughts you will have, and God's divine purpose will become clear.

2nd Peter 3:18 (NKJV) says,

> **"But grow in grace, and in the knowledge of our Lord and Saviour Jesus Christ. To Him be the glory both now and forever. Amen."**

When you struggle to forgive…

> *Mark 11:25 (NKJV) "And whenever you stand praying, if you have anything against anyone, forgive him, that your Father in heaven may also forgive you your trespasses."*

These are some of the warning signs that indicate you are struggling with unforgiveness in your life:

1. **You have uncontrollable outbursts of anger.** Someone says something or does something to you, and you find yourself lashing out at that person for no real reason. This person may not be the one who wounded you, but you make them the scapegoat for your anger.

2. **You become petty and impulsive.** You may find that you make cutting or snide remarks about, or even to, the person you have not forgiven. Your communication becomes aggressive, rude, and abrupt. Your unforgiveness causes you to want to control the person or the situation, to dominate or demean the other person.

3. **You refuse to take responsibility for your feelings and your actions.** By withholding forgiveness, you are holding the other person responsible, not just for initially wounding you, but for your reactions and behavior as well. You subconsciously are saying that they are responsible for your actions and unhappiness.

4. **You find yourself ill.** Holding on to unforgiveness, may lead to certain types of stress related illnesses like anxiety, depression, sleeplessness, arthritis, ***Proverbs 17:22 (NKJV), "A merry heart does good, like medicine, But a broken spirit dries the bones,"*** high blood pressure, and possibly certain autoimmune diseases. "Forgiveness Therapy" may help to alleviate some of these symptoms.

5. **You are keeping a list of offenses.** You are keeping a mental log of every perceived offensive word, action, avoidance, and every imaginable wrongdoing by the other person. You make this list your justification for your actions towards the offender.

6. **You constantly replay the offense in your mind.** You find yourself meditating on the events from days, and, sometimes, even years ago, that wounded you. With each replay of the event, the unforgiveness deepens and begins to effect areas of your life. The hurt of a broken relationship causes you to reject

every relationship. The betrayal of a friend causes you to isolate yourself and avoid friendships. The results of this behavior can be endless.

7. **You begin to gossip and slander the other person(s).** In retaliation, you begin to divulge things that had been shared in confidence. Your goal is to bring hurt to the other person. You become the evil person that you perceive the offender to be.

8. **You are unable to forgive yourself for your past failures or mistakes.** Often, the hardest person to forgive is yourself. I have struggled with this. I have replayed in my head, with detailed emotional horror, some of my failures. I have often heard myself say, "You are so stupid, stupid, stupid! What is wrong with you?" However, I have learned to CHOOSE TO FORGIVE myself, and not stay stuck in this cycle. *Proverbs 24:16 says that, "For a righteous man may fall seven times and rise again…"*

   1 John 1:9 (NKJV), "If we confess our sins, He is faithful and just to forgive us our sins and to cleanse us from all unrighteousness."

   COLOSSIANS 3:13 (NKJV) "Bearing with one another, and forgiving one another, if anyone has a complaint against another; even as Christ forgave you, so you also must do."

Luke 6:35-36 (NKJV) "But love your enemies, do good, and lend, hoping for nothing in return; and your reward will be great, and you will be sons of the Most High. For He is kind to the unthankful and evil. Therefore be merciful, just as your Father also is merciful."

You are accomplishing things, but you are not happy.

Personal achievement has become the cornerstone of American culture. Parents often want their children to do more and be better than the parents have achieved. They push their children to "be the best", "always win", causing the children to believe that their value as a person is measured by their achievements. Although the parents do not intend to, they are sending a message to their child that *who they are* is not enough. The child learns to define himself or herself by what they have done and can do, and not being who God created them to be.

Happiness is eternal, it is your attitude towards life and it occurs when your expectations meet your reality

These "Unhappy Achievers" find their self-esteem comes almost entirely from outside of themselves, it is based on the recognition and approval of others. They may be successful in their careers, but they are empty, self-focused individuals,

Happiness is eternal, it is your attitude towards life and it occurs when your expectations meet your reality.

driven to meet goals and deadlines, but unable to develop meaningful relationships. They are broken and wounded, needing to be made whole.

Psalms 34:18 (NLT), The LORD is close to the brokenhearted; he rescues those whose spirits are crushed.

There is an article on The Neurotypical Site, that was written on Maslow's Hierarchy of Basic Needs, in which a psychological study was conducted on happy, self-fulfilled humans by Psychologist Abraham Maslow. Maslow found that there are five levels of needs to be satisfied and self-fulfilled people constantly get all five of these needs met. Those five levels are.

Level 1: Physical Survival Needs

Need for food, drink, shelter, sleep and oxygen.

Level 2: Physical Safety Needs

Need to feel safe in the world: to feel safe from personal danger and threats.

Level 3: Love and Belonging Needs

Once the physical survival and safety needs scare being met, a need for love, affection and belonging begin to emerge. Maslow states: "The person…will hunger for affectionate relationships with people in general for a place in the group." Some of these needs include:

- ❖ *Family or belonging- the need to belong to a group, family, religion, town or class.*

- ❖ *Acceptance and understanding- the need to feel alright and to know that others accept you as you are.*

- ❖ *Loving and affection- the need both to get and give love.*

- ❖ *Intimacy- the need to share inner thoughts with others in close, caring ways.*

Level 4: Self-esteem Needs

Need to feel valued and to count for something. The need for confidence and recognition from others.

Level 5: Self-fulfilled (Self-actualized)

If the first four levels of needs are being met, then the fifth one will develop. The need for self-fulfillment. To become more what a person can be: to develop all aspects-physical, social, emotional, and spiritual. Among the characteristics of self-fulfilled people is awareness of living, completeness, joyfulness, unforgettable moments or periods of joy, unity and understanding.

CHAPTER 2

HOW DO WE GO THROUGH THE HEALING PROCESS?

ASK YOURSELF, "DO I WANT TO BE MADE WHOLE?"

IN ORDER TO BE healed, you must want to be made whole. That's why Jesus asked, "Do you want to be made whole?" He saw the condition, but he also saw the mental state of individuals. In order to be made whole, you must understand the process of releasing what has held you back.

In the book of *John 5: 2-9 (NKJV)*, I'm reminded of the story that talks about a man that was at the pool of Bethesda. This man had been lying there ill for 38 years, which says, *"Now there is at Jerusalem by the sheep market a pool, which is called in the Hebrew tongue Bethesda, having five porches. In these lay a great multitude of impotent folk, of blind, halt, withered, waiting for the moving of the water. For an angel went down at a certain season into the pool, and troubled the water: whosoever then first after troubling of the water stepped in was made whole of whatsoever disease he had. And a certain man was there, which had an infirmity thirty and eight years. When Jesus saw him lie, and knew that he had been now a long time in that case, he saith unto him, Wilt thou be made whole? The impotent man answered him, Sir, I have no man, when the water is troubled, to put me into the pool: but while I am coming, another steppeth down before me. Jesus saith unto him, Rise, take up they bed, and walk. And immediately the man was made whole, and took up his bed, and walked: and on the same day was the sabbath.*

There is a difference between being made "well" and being made "whole". "Well" is a temporary situation or condition, while "whole" is the totality of your life, beginning with your mentality. In chapter five, verse 7 the man had replied to Jesus by saying, ***"Sir, I have no man, when the water is troubled, to put me into the pool: but while I am coming, another steppeth down before me"*** and in verse 8, Jesus said to him, ***"Rise, take up thy bed, and walk."*** When Jesus had asked the man if he wanted to be made whole, the man did not say "Yes." Instead, he came with an excuse and had said that he had no one to help him into the pool. This man had a one-dimensional thought pattern and he thought that he needed help from someone to restore him. He did not know that Jesus was the Master Physician, who needs no assistance, and that His words alone would heal and restore.

Never leave the welfare of your internal state in the hands of anyone before God.

In the Bible, it states that the pool of Bethesda had many ill people among the porches. But Jesus focused on this one man, because He knew that he had been in that state for 38 years. Many theologians believe that this man could have been praying that God would do something for him. However, in 38 years nothing had happened, and no one was giving him the help he needed to get into the pool. It's possible the man thought no one cared about him. When Jesus asked him the question, ***"Wilt thou be made whole?"*** the man's response was that he had no one to help him. Imagine being ill for 38 years and not having anyone to help you. This confirms that this man was wounded, because he felt no one cared about his condition. He was scarred. However, Jesus wanted him not only to be healed and well, but to be made whole.

In the book of ***Luke chapter 8 (NKJV)***, it bears the story of the woman that had the issue of blood for over 12 years. The Bible says that when she touched the hem of His garment, in verse 48, He said to her, ***"Daughter, be of good comfort: "thy faith hath made thee whole; go in peace."*** This was a woman who had also been scarred, because she was identified as "The woman with the issue of blood." In the Levitical Law, when a woman was on her cycle or if she was bleeding, she had to be put away, and not be touched by anyone. This woman was scarred, she was hurt, because she felt rejected by all, given that she had been identified as the woman with the issue of blood. However, when she touched the hem of Jesus' garment, Jesus re-identified her. He said it openly, He said, "Woman, thou hath be made whole."

Never leave the welfare of your internal state in the hands of anyone before God.

Many times, we think back and look at our lives and say, "Does anybody care?"; "Do they even see me?"; and "Do they love me?" I think we all have said those words at one point in our lives, when we felt unappreciated or when we felt like no one cared about us. I have personally experienced this when I preach. The enemy tries to put negative thoughts in my head, such as, "They don't care about me" or "They don't know what I'm going through." That is when I tell the enemy, "Enemy, I'm not doing it for them, I'm doing it for my Father in heaven, because I'm called to do it! I am about my Father's business."

You cannot let your past and those who have mocked you dictate your future and your language. You have nothing to prove to them, because your conduct should match your confession. People will see when God has brought you out of the darkness and into His marvelous light. His hand over your life speaks for itself. However, you must be willing to ask yourself if you want to be made whole.

YOU MUST STOP SIPPING ON BITTERNESS

Ephesians 4:31-32 (NKJV, "Let all bitterness, wrath, anger, clamor, and evil speaking be put away from you, with all malice. And be kind to one another, tenderhearted, forgiving one another, even as God in Christ forgave you."

The Oxford dictionary defines bitterness as, "anger and disappointment at being treated unfairly; resentment." Bitterness can be more destructive than anger, because it leads to feeling helpless. In psychological terms, it is referred to as embitterment. This happens when a you feel there is no action left for you to take. Everything seems to be out of your control. This can happen with a failed relationship, death of a loved one or pet, or even when you are repeatedly passed for a promotion on the job, etc. As bitterness entraps your emotion and consumes your thoughts, depression can set in.

Whatever you think about the most, will grow.

Bitterness causes you to continually meditate on and repeat what people have said about you. You begin to make excuses like, "You don't understand what I have had to go through," or "Everyone that was around me was negative," or "My father was an addict or alcoholic or abusive," etc. This is sipping on

Whatever you think about the most, will grow.

bitterness. It must be stopped! The past is over! You must choose to break those generational cycles.

I sipped on bitterness. I was frustrated. I wanted to prove to the world that I wasn't a person who learned slowly or had "special needs." I wanted the people from my past to regret the negative words they had spoken over my life. I wanted to make them hurt like they had hurt me. Then, I heard God say to me, "Son, you must forgive them. Stop sipping on this bitterness, because the devil has you stuck." If you continue to focus on the past hurts, you will not be able to advance in life. You may advance diminutively, but your heart will not be right with God. You will grow angry and resentful. ***Hebrews 12:5 (ESV), "See to it that no one fails to obtain the grace of God; that no ROOT OF BITTERNESS springs up and causes trouble, and by it many become defiled.***" The Good News is, you don't have to stay where you are! You have a Father in Heaven who wants to see all your scars healed.

I am reminded of the story of Cain and Abel found in ***Genesis 4:1-16***. Cain became consumed with anger and bitterness towards God and his brother Abel. God had found Abel's sacrifice of the first fruit and his flock more acceptable than Cain's sacrifice of his harvested fruit and vegetable. God told Cain essentially to let it go and get it right the next time. But Cain allowed the anger and bitterness to grow into hatred, and he killed his brother.

God would have healed Cain's heart if he had relinquished his anger and sought God's forgiveness.

2 Corinthians 5:17 (KJV) says,

> *"Therefore if any man be in Christ, he is a new creature; old things have passed away; behold, all things are become new."*

So why do we talk about the past if all things have become new? When the bitterness and anger have been healed, our past wounds and scars are transformed into our testimony of victory and praise to help others get set free! ***Revelation 12:11 (NKJV), "And they overcame him by the blood of the Lamb, and by the word of their testimony..."*** I had to learn that my past has nothing to do with my future. I grew to realize that my God loves me so much, that my past could not kill or stop God's plans and purposes for my life.

THREE WAYS TO START DEALING WITH BITTERNESS

1. **Do a serious re-evaluation.** Bitterness thrives on sympathy. Oftentimes, when we are speaking to someone about a certain situation that may have occurred, we start lying to ourselves about what really happened and what is truly upsetting us in an effort to gain their sympathy.

    Psalms 55:22 (NKJV), "Cast your burden on the LORD, And He shall sustain you; He shall never permit the righteous to be moved."

2. **Face your hidden fears.** Are you fearful of what others think of you? Of not being worthy, of betrayal, of failure?

3. **Step into the now.** Bitterness is fed when we dwell on the "awful thing that happened" to us, and fantasize revenge against the perpetrator (s), or we

meditate on where we would be if things had gone differently.

CHAPTER 4

YOU MUST FORGIVE

Romans 5:8 (NKJV) "But God demonstrates His own love toward us, in that while we were still sinners, Christ died for us."

IN ORDER TO BE completely whole, you must come to the realization that the Bible tells us the battles are not ours, but the Lord's. You should not hold unforgiveness in your heart. I know how difficult that can be. I experienced deep wounds in my life, but I had to release them.

By the age of 4 years old, my mother and father had separated and divorced. From that time on, my father would be in and out of my life. He tried to act like everything was ok, instead of addressing why he had not been more involved in my life. I carried a great deal of bitterness towards him, because of the promises he broke. My father would plan to take me for a weekend, but never show up, leaving me with my suitcases packed, looking out the window, waiting for his car to pull up in the driveway.

My father came back into my life when I was 23, wanting to reconcile with me. He apologized for hurting me. He said he was seeking God for answers to his life. I told him that I forgave him, but, deep inside, I didn't release him to the Lord. I spoke the right words saying, "I had forgiven him," but the scars and wounds I carried did not agree with what I had spoken. This dawned on me when I became engaged to be married. I was 25 years old when I introduced my father to my fiancé. He actually told her that I wasn't ready to get married! He said my life showed my immaturity. I immediately became irate, and, in a very pointed way, told him that he didn't know who I was! "How dare he assume that I wasn't ready for marriage." He had been absent almost my whole life, and he had the audacity to tell my future wife that I wasn't ready to be her husband! At that point, anger and frustration rose up in me towards my father. My fiancé noticed the change in my emotions. She began to explain to me that I was holding on to unforgiveness. I realized my fiancé was right. I had spoken the words saying that I had forgiven him, but I had never released my anger towards him. The wounds and the scars were still there, and I had to address the situation.

Healing begins at the point of exposure.

Once I faced my deep woundedness, I had to approach my father, and tell him how I felt. I was able to tell him that even though he had apologized to me, I was still angry at him for not being in my life to help me identify who I was to become and to exemplify what a man's role was to be. You see, a father is called to "imprint" their sons and daughters, by guidance and role modeling a Godly lifestyle. This imprinting is much like a fingerprint which allows for identifying a specific person. My father, by his absence and lack of involvement in my life, had denied me of that.

Healing begins at the point of exposure

Instead, I grew up in the streets with the fingerprint of the world identifying me. I ended up making a lot of bad decisions. I was looking for a father to tell me who I was, who I was to be. My anger and unforgiveness towards my father had become very deep. However, the day I exposed my heart to him, we both ended in tears. He admitted to me that because of his bad decisions, he had felt inadequate and incapable of being a father to me, so he chose to avoid me. He did not have Christ in his life at the time to bring him out of his mess, so he had stayed away. We both ended up crying profusely, sincerely sorry for our mistakes and wrong attitudes towards each other. The Holy Spirit came into our midst and brought healing to our broken relationship. At that moment, the wounds of my past began to heal.

THREE BENEFITS OF FORGIVING

> *Colossians 3:13 (NKJV), "Forbearing one another, and forgiving one another, if any man have a quarrel against any: even as Christ forgave you, so also do ye."*

1. **When you forgive, you detach your emotions from your pain.**

When you haven't forgiven, your emotions will be overly displayed, and people will see that there's something still bothering you. Have you ever looked at someone, and you could see that they were upset? They probably didn't even realize that everything they were feeling internally was being expressed externally. Your emotions can be seen in your facial features and heard in your speech or observed in your body language as well. However, when you forgive, you are detaching your emotions from your pain. You know that God said that the battle is not yours, but His.

Forgiveness is freedom.

> *Psalms 105:15 (NKJV), "Saying, Touch not mine anointed, and do my prophets no harm."*

In the past, I was working in sales. The people I worked with knew that I was a Pastor, and they mocked me daily for it. They would tease me by saying, "Pastor, so how much money did you make in the collection

Forgiveness is freedom.

today?" Another co-worker would then put on a show for everyone, dancing and making overly exaggerating expressions of a pastor preaching. The thing that offended me most, was their mocking of my culture. While they taunted me, the Lord said to me, "Are you going to respond to that?" I then responded to Him, "No, Lord." Then I heard Him say to me, "Good, because if you know who you are, there shouldn't be a response." The mocking and teasing went on for months. Then they became very jealous of me, because God had elevated me to the top grossing salesman. In their jealousy, the other salesmen, as God had told me, tried to say that I was "being a con artist." I kept my mouth shut, even though I wanted to say something to them. I got to the point where I felt this urge to hit them, but God… I would smile and say, "No, that's not who I am," and would walk away. God was teaching me to take my "peace of mind" off the life support of others' acceptance or approval, by refusing to let them tell me what I could and could not do.

After some time passed, I was given my own office, but that still didn't stop my co-workers from the ongoing mocking. The mocking gradually stopped as they saw how well I was doing. That is when they started coming to me, seeking council and asking about my success. They began to ask me how they could get my same results in their sales. They were acting more friendly, even asking how my day was going. I would respond to them and give God the credit for an outstanding day. I began to minister to them, explaining to them that it wasn't about how good I was in sales, but that all the credit was due to God's hand on my life. As God opened the doors of expressing my success, I was able to share that prayer was the key of releasing the abundance of blessings, because I acknowledged Him as my provider. They wanted what I had, so I showed them. God changed the atmosphere in this company! Even though I am no longer with the company, there are still over 100 people praying every morning.

> *Philippians 4:19 (AMPC), "And my God will liberally supply (fill to the full) your every need according to His riches in glory in Christ Jesus."*

You need to remember, that you don't need accolades from people. You don't need to be liked on social media, because you are the chosen of God. He loves you! The favor of God is called to be evident in your life, and when it happens, God will draw people to you with whom you can share Jesus.

2.   **You make your heart available for newer and better.**

> *"Do not remember the former things, Nor consider the things of old. Behold, I will do a new thing, Now it shall spring forth; Shall you not know it? I will even make a road in the wilderness And rivers in the desert." Isaiah 43:18-19 (NKJV)*

When you hold on to frustration and unforgiveness, it hinders you from achieving self-fulfillment. You must want to make your heart available for "newer and better;" and the only way that can happen is if you focus on healing from your fragmented past. ***Psalms 147:3 (NKJV) says, "He heals the brokenhearted and binds up their wounds."*** God will not allow your brokenness to spread. He will bind it up. He will make sure it is sustained. The more you come to understand the time you have been given on Earth, the more you will start to speak like Jesus, saying, "I must be about my Father's business." You will realize that you cannot let life's issues and circumstances hinder what God is saying about your purpose."

In the Bible we are given an example of a broken woman, a woman who was rejected, wounded and scarred. She overcame her scars by making her heart available for "newer and better." This woman was from Samaria and her story can be found in the book of ***John 4:6-30 (NKJV), it says, "Now Jacob's well was there. Jesus therefore, being wearied from His journey, sat thus by the well. It was about the sixth hour. A woman of Samaria came to draw water. Jesus said to her, "Give Me a drink." For His disciples had gone away into the city to buy food. Then the woman of Samaria said to Him, "How is it that You, being a Jew, ask a drink from me, a Samaritan woman?" For Jews have no dealings with Samaritans. Jesus answered and said to her, "If you knew the gift of God, and who it is who says to you, 'Give***

Me a drink,' you would have asked Him, and He would have given you living water." The woman said to Him, "Sir, You have nothing to draw with, and the well is deep. Where then do You get that living water? Are You greater than our father Jacob, who gave us the well, and drank from it himself, as well as his sons and his livestock?" Jesus answered and said to her, "Whoever drinks of this water will thirst again, but whoever drinks of the water that I shall give him will never thirst. But the water that I shall give him will become in him a fountain of water springing up into everlasting life." The woman said to Him, "Sir, give me this water, that I may not thirst, nor come here to draw." Jesus said to her, "Go, call your husband, and come here." The woman answered and said, "I have no husband." Jesus said to her, "You have well said, 'I have no husband,' for you have had five husbands, and the one whom you now have is not your husband; in that you spoke truly." The woman said to Him, "Sir, I perceive that You are a prophet. Our fathers worshiped on this mountain, and you Jews say that in Jerusalem is the place where one ought to worship." Jesus said to her, "Woman, believe Me, the hour is coming when you will neither on this mountain, nor in Jerusalem, worship the Father. You worship what you do not know; we know what we worship, for salvation is of the Jews. But the hour is coming, and now is, when the true worshipers will worship the Father in spirit and truth; for the Father is seeking such to worship Him. God is Spirit, and those who worship Him must worship in spirit and truth."

The woman said to Him, "I know that Messiah is coming" (who is called Christ). "When He comes, He will tell us all things." Jesus said to her, "I who speak to you am He." And at this point His disciples came, and they marveled that He talked with a woman; yet no one said, "What do You seek?" or, "Why are You talking with her?" The woman then left her waterpot, went her way into the city, and said to the men, "Come, see a Man who told me all things that I ever did. Could this be the Christ?" Then they went out of the city and came to Him.

After reading the context of this message, we find that the Samaritan woman had a problem with past relationships. Having been married five times. Keep in mind, that in Biblical times, it was prohibited for a woman to request a divorce from her husband, only the men could divorce their wives. Imagine what the Samaritan woman felt, being divorced five times, which meant being rejected by five men. Jesus had confronted the Samaritan woman that the man she was living with was not her husband. Could it be that she was living in fear that she would once again be rejected? Were her scars strangling her future?

Scars are meant to strangle your future.

The story of the Samaritan woman at the well teaches us that God loves us despite our destitute lives. God values us enough to actively seek us, to welcome us into intimacy, and to rejoice in our worship to him. When Jesus met the Samaritan woman at the well, he had intentionally pulled away from his disciples, knowing that she would be there at that appointed time. It was a very rare occasion, because He and the Samaritan woman were alone, with no disciples or large crowds. It was just Jesus and this woman, having a conversation. This could be considered a therapeutic session, because of the woman's problems in her relationships. She was coming from a place of brokenness, pain, and rejection, never having a real genuine relationship.

Jesus shared with her that God wanted "newer and better" for her. Jesus spoke to her about coming to God, in spirit and in truth. After her conversation with Jesus, the Samaritan woman's heart was healed. She opened her heart to "newer and better" by having a genuine relationship with God. ***John 4:23, (NLT), "But the time is coming—indeed it's here now—when true worshipers will worship the Father in spirit and in truth. The Father is looking for those who will worship him that way."*** Only through Jesus, can we obtain and receive eternal life; ***John 4:13-14 Jesus answered and said to her, "Whoever drinks of this water will thirst again, but whoever drinks of the water that I shall give him will never thirst. But the water that I shall give him will become in him a fountain of water springing up into everlasting life."***

3.   You align your heart with God.

Luke 23:34 (NKJV), Jesus said, "Father forgive them, for they know not what they do…"

To align your heart with God, means you are saying, "God, I forgive them." I had to come to the realization that my father did not know what he was doing, and that I needed to forgive him. When I forgave him, I aligned myself with God, and He reminded me that He forgave us, so I must forgive others as well.

When you forgive, you and god are on the same page. Aligning with God is the secret to real deliverance from heartbreak.

I remember the vinyl music albums we used to listen to. When they would become scratched, the needle would stick in scratch. The only way you could stop it from being stuck, was to bump the needle out of the scratch. That meant you had to go to the player to move the needle. If you didn't move the needle, it was going to stay stuck, and repeat the same music over and over, unable to move on. Well God says, "Get up and move the needle!" Destiny awaits you, and you cannot let scars and wounds of the soul keep you from moving forward. You must get up!

I'm convinced with all my heart that scars were never meant to stay as scars, they were meant to be stars. Stars for other people to glean from. God said to me, "the scars of your heart can be the roadmap to freedom for somebody." When you tell people how you were delivered and set free, you will be giving them an opportunity to be set free themselves. We know that all things work together for better, and God doesn't want you to stay stuck in negative situations. He will make the scar become a star for His glory, so that someone else will be delivered, just as you were delivered.

I believe that we need to begin to release the hurt and pain in our lives. There are a lot of people that say they have released unforgiveness, but their scars are so sensitive, they misunderstand what someone says, causing them to breakdown. We, who have been healed of our scars, must lovingly speak the truth of God's love for them, His plans for their life, and help them get back on the same page with God.

YOU MUST ADOPT SAFE RELATIONSHIPS

> *Proverbs 11:14 (NKJV), "Where there is no counsel, the people fall; but in the multitude of counselors there is safety."*

One of the greatest components of healing is to be relational. It's critical that you have the right people around you, especially Godly positive people. When you have Godly people around you, they will have a passion and a hunger for God. Sometimes the strongest tactics and the easiest way forward is to accept new relationships. You must cut off the unhealthy relationships first, to develop the healthy ones. Godly relationships should be a safety net, a stable place to go to. The Hebrew word *shalem*, which translates as *safe* in English, means- full, made ready, peaceable, stable and whole. Therefore, that "safety net," is the wholeness, the peace and the stability you need to promote healing.

> ***Luke 4:18 (AMP) says, "The Spirit of the LORD is upon Me, Because He has anointed Me To preach the gospel to the poor; He has sent Me [a]to heal the brokenhearted, To proclaim liberty to the captives And recovery of sight to the blind, To set at liberty those who are oppressed."***

Jesus said I am anointed to heal the brokenhearted, and to liberate those who are bruised. Bruising speaks of an internal injury caused by a trauma of some kind. Many times, it is not even visible on the exterior, but nevertheless it is painful. Some people are anointed to liberate those that are bruised. Some are anointed to heal the brokenhearted. Many times, that anointing came through their own wounds, scars, and healing process.

If your relationships have been corrupted with verbal abuse, causing negative thinking, such as, "I'll never be able to do this."; "Why is this always happening to me?";

"Something is wrong with me"; then leave that atmosphere. You cannot advance if you are surrounded with negativity and abuse.

After my healing of unforgiveness took place, I was determined to break the stronghold of words that had scarred me. I sought educational opportunities to expand my thinking and challenged my comprehension. By studying new words and their meanings, my vocabulary expanded, and I surrounded myself with people who excelled in their education. For there is power in associations, because it determines your acceleration or stagnation.

My life then began to spiral upwards. When I was 35 years old, I ran into my former 6th grade teacher. The teacher recalled that I had been classified as "special needs" by the education system and was shocked at how much I had achieved. Today, I have two doctorate degrees, I am a college professor at Arizona, U.S.A Christian University, an entrepreneur, a life coach, overseer of multiple ministries, own an automobile dealership, and pastor a growing church in Avondale, Arizona. I believed who God said I was and what I could do in Christ, and I did not allow people's opinions, or the education system define what I could or could not do. I have become the man I am today because I learned to listen to God and obey Him. I am no longer holding on to my past.

I have a passion for speaking to people who are broken and hurting, because I've been a hurt and broken person. I've been delivered and set free from all traumatization of my past. I desire to give support and direction and help bring healing to those who are where I once was. If you are where I was, broken and scarred, do not give up, do not stop pressing for God's best for you. You are a child of God, and God has given you the Holy Spirit! He is the most influential being that exists, and He dwells inside of you. He will guide you to the "newer and better" you that God created you to be!

> *The scars on your heart, can be the roadmap to freedom for somene else.*

Philippians 4:6-7 (NKJV), "Be anxious for nothing, but in everything by prayer and supplication, with thanksgiving, let your requests be made known to God; and the peace of God, which surpasses all understanding, will guard your hearts and minds through Christ Jesus.

John 3:17, For God did not send the Son into the world in order to judge (to reject, to condemn, to pass sentence on) the world, but that the world might find salvation and be made safe and sound through Him.

Conclusion

T HE BIBLE PRESENTS TO us many people who, in spite of what they went through, were able to serve the Lord, even after going through their own phase of being scarred and broken. Their examples will teach us how God mends a broken heart into wholeness and will inspire us to allow God to use us despite of our past. Let us look at a few biblical characters…

1. JOSEPH

Joseph was a dreamer, famous for his colorful coat, a proud young man, with a legacy as Egypt's administrator. He had so many heartbreaking moments, between the coat, his family, and the government of Egypt. He was abused by his brothers and sold as a slave to Egypt. He was falsely accused of sexually harassing his master's wife, thrown in prison, and forgotten by friends who should've helped him in return for a favor, and was again thought of wrongly by his brothers when they were reunited. After all he went through, we would understand if Joseph would have become a cynical man who hated his family and wanted revenge against all who hurt him. No, he didn't allow himself to succumb to those standards. What was his secret? He forgave.

> **Genesis 50:20, "But as for you, you meant evil against me; but God meant it for good, in order to bring it about as it is this day, to save many people alive.**

2.   DAVID

Young David, destined to sit on the throne of Israel after King Saul, had to run away, because Saul felt threatened by him. Saul wanted David dead. David had served Saul faithfully: he slew Goliath, ministered to Saul in his chambers, was the husband to Saul's daughter, Michal, served as a captain in Saul's army, and was best friends with Saul's son, Jonathon. He never wronged Saul, but Saul wanted to kill him. David even had the chance to slay Saul, but he did not. Instead, David loved Saul and continued to honor him. Even after David became King, he would take Jonathan's son, Mephibosheth, to sit at the King's master table, and to be cared for. David chose to forgive Saul and walk as an upright man before God.

2 Samuel 9:6-7, Now when Mephibosheth, the son of Jonathan, the son of Saul, had come to David, he fell on his face and prostrated himself. Then David said, "Mephibosheth?" And he answered, "Here is your servant!" So David said to him, "Do not fear, for I will surely show you kindness for Jonathan your father's sake, and will restore to you all the land of Saul your grandfather; and you shall eat bread at my table continually."

2.   LEAH (Genesis 29:15-35)

The story about Leah records that Jacob, the son of Isaac, was sent by his father to his Uncle Laban's homeland to find a bride. Jacob had encountered Rachel, one of Laban's daughters, upon arrival, and immediately was attracted to her. The Bible tells us that Rachel was shapely and had a lovely face. He negotiated with Laban to work seven years for the privilege of marrying the woman he loved. The time went by quickly as Jacob anticipated his wedding to Rachel. When the wedding day arrived, Laban, who was a deceitful man and a master con man, helped his son-in-law to drink lots of wine and then sent his older daughter, Leah, into the bridal chamber. Leah's face was veiled according to the marriage custom and Jacob, in his altered condition, consummated his marriage with Leah and not his beloved Rachel. You see, it was the custom of the land that the older sister had to marry first, so Laban made sure that happened.

However, Jacob did not have any attraction or love for Leah. When Jacob realized what Laban had done, Jacob was furious! Laban agreed to give him Rachel as his wife, after the seven-day wedding period, in exchange for another seven years of labor. *(Genesis 29:27, NKJV)*

Leah was caught in the middle of Laban's manipulation and deception. She was married to a man who was madly in love with her younger sister and rejected by him. She was the victim of her father's treachery, and she was placed in competition with her beautiful younger sister. All Leah wanted was to be loved, admired and respected for who she was. Her husband's rejection wounded and scarred her deeply and could have made her bitter and resentful. However, God saw Leah's pain and blessed her to give birth to six of Jacob's sons. The names of her son's indicate the pain that she felt. However, when she delivered her fourth son, God was bringing her healing. She named him Judah, which means, "Let Jehovah be praised!" Leah found her fulfillment in Jehovah God and began to praise Him, and in her praise, she found herself in the presence of God! Leah was chosen by God to carry the seed of the future Messiah, the Lion of the tribe of Judah! God sees you in praise. God hears you in praise. God will make you whole and restore your heart in the midst of praising Him!

Leah had come to realize she couldn't get Jacobs attention, and that he would always prefer Rachel. She recognized it was time to change her direction and turn to God. When you are fed up with people not wanting you around and rejecting you, you must shift your mind!

3.   GOMER (Hosea Chapters 1-3)

Gomer was the wife of the prophet Hosea. She was a harlot (prostitute), and God told his prophet to marry her as a visual representation to the people of Israel of their relationship with Him. The Bible does not tell us what events in Gomer's life had caused her to become a harlot, but we can safely assume that there were traumatizing circumstances that drove her to that profession. Gomer's scars and woundedness were so deep, that after several years of being married to Hosea, she ran away and went back into prostitution. Hosea could have chosen to feel humiliated, hurt, rejected by Gomer, but he listened to God and went after his rebellious wife. *Hosea 3:1 (NLT)*, *"Go and love your wife again, even though she commits adultery with another lover."* He again redeemed Gomer from her life of prostitution and took her back into his home to love and care for her. You see, Hosea's name means "salvation," and God was showing Israel, and ultimately all of us, just how great His love is toward His chosen ones.

Just like Gomer, millions of people have experienced traumatic life events, leaving them scarred and wounded. Traumatic events affect the physical and emotional (psyche) areas. The person's sense of well-being, security, dignity, their feelings about themselves, and the will to live can be dramatically altered. Psychological studies have shown that children who have experienced a traumatic event, who are asked to draw a picture showing how they feel, will usually draw a heart that is broken or wounded in some way. It may have a crack in it, lines drawn through it, tears or blood dripping from it, but it shows their deep woundedness.

When we focus on and keep rehearsing the events and words and attitudes of others towards us, the wound cannot heal. The scar becomes larger and uglier. Remember, Gomer, went back to her past life of harlotry. But God had Hosea forgive her again and love her to wholeness, to illustrate that His great love for each of us individually is the answer to our healing and wholeness.

Jesus will not leave us in our broken, scarred conditions. He emptied His life on the cross to bring us back to our Father. Jesus is our Savior! He was broken so that we could be made whole. *(Isaiah 53:5-8)*

Our lives move in the direction of our most dominant thoughts.

4.   JESUS CHRIST THE MESSIAH

Jesus came to His own, and they rejected Him. *(John 1:11)* He came to the people of Israel, seeking to save those who were lost. *(Luke 18:1)* He loved them. He fed them. He healed them. He taught them about His Father's Kingdom. But they rejected Him, betrayed Him, and demanded that the Roman government crucify him on a cross as a condemned criminal. Yes, this was His Father's plan from before the beginning of the earth. *(Revelation 13:8)* Jesus had come do His Father's will and become the perfect, spotless sacrifice required to cover the sins of the world. He was rejected. He was beaten beyond recognition. He was tortured and hung on a cross. He poured out His life's blood, so that the very ones doing this to Him, and all mankind forever, could be saved. *(Hebrews 9:22, AMP)* God, required Jesus to forgive the one's crucifying Him before Jesus could declare that "It is Finished." *Luke 23:34 (NKJV), "He said, 'Father, forgive them, for they do not know what they do...'"*

It is Christ's forgiveness on the cross, once received, that brings spiritual wholeness. It is His love and example, that teaches us to forgive those who have broken and scarred us, so that we can become whole emotionally. Only God, through the Holy Spirit, can guide us through the process of healing. That healing cannot begin until we choose to forgive the ones who wounded us.

I pray that this book has brought you to an awareness that all of us are scarred in some way. God is the healer. God desires that we all be made whole.

> ***John 2:2, (AMP), "Beloved, I pray that in every way you may succeed and prosper and be in good health (physically), just as (I know) your soul prospers (spiritually)."***

Healing Verses

Jeremiah 30:17 (NLT)

"I will give you back your health and heal your wounds," says the Lord. For you are called and outcast-Jerusalem for whom no one cares.

Jeremiah 17:14 (NKJV)

Heal me, O Lord, and I shall be healed; save me, and I shall be saved: for thou art my praise.

Jeremiah 33:6 (NLT)

"Nevertheless, the time will come when I will heal, Jerusalem's wounds and give it prosperity and true peace."

Jeremiah 3:22 (NKJV)

Return, ye backsliding children, and I will heal your backslidings. Behold, we come unto thee; for thou art the Lord our God.

Exodus 23:25 (NKJV)

And ye shall serve the Lord your God, and he shall bless thy bread, and thy water; and I will take sickness away from the midst of thee.

Isaiah 53:5 (NLT)

But he was pierced for our

rebellion, crushed for our sins. He was beaten so we could be whole. He was whipped so we could be healed.

Luke 1:37 (NKJV)
For with God nothing shall be impossible.

Luke 18:27 (NKJV)
And he said, The things which are impossible with men are possible with God.

James 5:13 (NLT)
Are any of you suffering hardships? You should pray. Are any of you happy? You should sing praises.

James 4:7 (NKJV)
Submit yourselves therefore to God. Resist the devil, and he will flee from you.

Hebrew 4:16 (NLT)
So let us come boldly to the throne of our gracious God. There we will receive his mercy, and we will find grace

to help us when we need it most.

Mark 10:27 (NLT)
Jesus looked at them intently and said, "Humanly speaking, it is impossible. But not with God. Everything is possible with God."

Psalm 30:2 (NKJV)
O Lord my God, thou hast brought up my soul from the grave: thou hast kept me alive, that I should not go down to the pit.

Psalm 147:3 (NKJV)
He health the broken in heart, and bindeth up their wounds.

Psalm 107:20 (NKJV)
He sent his word, and healed them, and delivered them from their destructions.

Psalm 34:19 (NLT)
The righteous person faces many troubles, but the Lord

comes to the rescue each time.

Psalm 51:12 (NLT)

Restore to me thy joy of your salvation, and make me willing to obey you.

Psalms 103:2-4 (NKJV)

Bless the Lord, O my soul, and forget not all his benefits: Who forgiveth all thine iniquities; who healeth all thy diseases; Who redeemeth thy life from destruction; who crowneth thee with loving kindness and tender mercies.

Proverbs 17:22

A cheerful heart is good medicine, but a broken spirit saps a person's strength.

Proverbs 3:7-8 (NLT)

Don't be impressed with your own wisdom. Instead, fear the Lord and turn away from evil. Then you will have healing for your body and strength for your bones.

Proverbs 16:24 (NKJV)

Pleasant words are as honeycomb, sweet to the soul, and health to the bones.

Proverbs 4:20-22 (NLT)

My child, pay attention to what I say. Listen carefully to my words. Don't lose sight of them. Let them penetrate deep into your heart, for they bring life to those who find them, and healing to their whole body.

Philippians 4:19 (NKJV)

But my God shall supply all your need according to his riches in glory by Christ Jesus.

Hosea 14:4 (NLT)

The Lord says, "Then I will heal you of your faithlessness; my love will know no bounds, for my anger will be gone forever.

Proverbs 12:18 (NLT)

Some people make cutting remarks, but the words of the wise bring healing.

Reflections

Reflections

Reflections

Reflections

www.ingramcontent.com/pod-product-compliance
Lightning Source LLC
Chambersburg PA
CBHW032128050726
47590CB00008B/3011